GW01454201

You couldn't write it 🤣

By Keith Healicon.

Copyright © Keith Healicon. All rights reserved.

No parts of this book may be reproduced or transmitted in any form or by any other means without the prior permission from the publisher. The right of Keith Healicon to be identified as the author of this book has been asserted by him in accordance with the Copyright, Designs and Patent Act 1988. First published in 2024.

ISBN-9798877840591

keithhealiconbooks@gmail.com

Foreword.

I wish I had been given a fiver for every time I have heard the phrase, 'You couldn't write it!'

As you will no doubt agree, actual true-to-life funny events, are far more comical than made up written jokes.

Like every person on this planet, I have personally experienced such hilarious true-life events. Whilst being a manager on Northern Rail, I met, interviewed and worked with many characters from across the North West. Some of these people are included in this book.

I have added a few of my family and friend's favourite experiences as well.

Here are twenty (plus a bonus), of my favourites. The grammar and language may not be perfect English. It's meant to be that way. The cartoons are far from perfect as well. I drew them 😃.

Thanks to Kam (book over) and Dan again (technical help), for their help.

Please enjoy.

Keith.

CONTENTS

THE LYING SCOUSER

I was required to carry out interviews for a vacant Train Presentation Supervisor (a posh title for a cleaning team leader), at Wigan Wallgate Train Station on behalf of Northern Rail. I did the interviews with a mate of mine Stevie G. Steve was one of the training officers at Newton Heath where I was based myself. I was required by company policy to carry out the interviews with another responsible person. Steve wanted some different interview experience from a different department. Plus, he wanted a laugh. He certainly had a laugh with me that day.

There is a small concourse at Wigan, with one train track running either side. On the concourse, there is a single-story building. This contains a small customer service enquiry room at the front, a train staff mess room in the middle, with the Regional Station Manager's (Joan at the time) office, at the end. The lovely Joan very kindly let me have use of the office for the day.

The office had recently been refurbished (unusual in itself for Wigan I know! But there you go). The rooms had no outside windows. The offices had recently been equipped with some new energy saving devices. One such energy saving system involved a motion sensor. In short, if someone entered the room, the sensor would activate the lights to come on. If there was no movement in the room for ten minutes or so, the sensor would deactivate the lights to automatically turn off. In our case, this happened a few times during the day. Either Steve or myself would stand up, raise a hand or walk. The lights would come back on, simple.

Our third interviewee of the day entered the office at eleven, mid-morning. Straight from the 'getco', he was a right arrogant cocky b*****d! A scouser called Billy. I nicknamed him Billy Bulls**t. Steve named him Billy Big B*****ks 😃.

He was twenty-six years old. He strutted into the office like a proud peacock. He was forever twitching his neck and smiling all the time, showing off his brilliant white teeth. He was loud and excitable. Steve and myself could not help but immediately look at each other. Billy was very smartly dressed. He had the most outrageous gelled combed-back jet-black hair style.

"Let's save time gentlemen!" Was his opening irritating statement. "I'm your man!" He held both arms out wide, palms facing us 😠.

To put it mildly, Billy did not create a very good first impression. He would have been better applying for a slot on Love Island rather than Northern Rail. He would have stood more chance.

As was normal practice, we started the interview with an informal chat. Obviously, Billy had done everything and been everywhere, even at the ripe old age of twenty-six. The interview had very quickly become farcical. He used the odd swear word, but we did not mind that, because so did we.

My colleague Steve became confused when I began the official interview. I started off by telling Billy that we were conducting the interview in a state-of-the-art new room recently invented by the Japanese 😲. From the corner of my eye, I could see Steve looking sideways at me.

I went on by telling Billy that if he told lies during the interview, all the lights would go off in the room. The penny now dropped with Steve.

Billy had already been in the office for several minutes. The lights had remained on. I asked my first question.

"Billy. Have you had any experience in being a team leader, you know, in supervising a team of people?"

Billy rapped his knuckles, clanging his two heavy gold rings on the table.

"Yep! I most certainly have!" He said in his confident scouse manner." I was in charge of fifty people in the Tesco stock factory in Liverpool".

The timing was absolutely perfect. It could not have gone any better!

Yes, you've guessed it! The lights went out, the room was in darkness.

I couldn't resist it 😈.

"You lying b*****d!" I roared out. Me and Steve remained in our seats in the darkened room.

Billy hesitated. "Well. I wasn't ACTUALLY in charge," Billy pleaded, digging his hole even deeper." I only stood in whilst the gaffer went to the dentist once. I did apply for his job though!"

Whilst we were still sat down in the dark, I told Billy to calm down.

"I DID tell you about the Japanese truth system Billy. Now let's get back on track."

The room was quiet, in total darkness, (although I'm sure I heard muffled sniggering from Steve).

"Right. What's your first name again?" I asked.

"Billy".

I stood up and waved my hands. Low and behold, the lights came back on.

I looked around. I don't know whose face was redder? Billy with embarrassment or Steve trying to hold himself together 😊.

YOU COULDN'T WRITE IT 😂.

CATH THE WIGAN HOOKER

After the hilarious farce of Billy, the lying scouser, (I honestly don't know to this day if he fully realised what had gone on that day), the next candidate in for the Train Cleaning Supervisor at Wigan was a lady called Cath.

Even before we got to Wigan, I was always going to give Cath the Supervisor position. Cath was in her late-forties. She had worked as a train cleaner at Wigan for five years. She was one of the best cleaners I have ever worked with 👌.

She was never sick. She was dead conscientious and she never let me down. She never complained. Even when working the long cold freezing nights at Wigan, cleaning the insides and outsides of the trains.

Two of Cath's many attributes were her personality and sense of humour. Every time I called on my regular visits, Cath would greet me with a beaming smile and a coffee exactly how I liked it. We would then spend a bit of time taking the p**s out of each other. Cath could not only stand her ground, but would give out more in return. We had a cracking working relationship 👌.

Cath was lesbian and slightly over-weight. (Me being very polite again). Let's just say, Cath was very cuddly. We always had a nice cuddle when meeting up, and another before I left.

Everybody at Wigan loved and respected Cath. The appointment was a no-brainer really.

Anyway, back to the story. Stevie G, my fellow interviewing colleague knew absolutely nothing about Cath. I purposely did not tell him. Steve was in for another little surprise.

Cuddly Cath entered the office just after dinner time. Pretending we didn't know each other, I stood up and introduced myself and Steve. Cath had recently had her short-spiked hair dyed cherry red. It matched her Wigan rugby league red and white striped top. Cath was an avid follower of her beloved Wigan rugby league club.

I started with my usual informal pre-interview chat. However, this one was slightly different. I started by telling her about the previous candidate, Bull***t Billy. Cath laughed her t**s off at the story. Steve was also laughing away, not for long though!

"Do you live local Cath?" I asked, knowing full-well exactly where she lived.

"Yes, just down the road. I have lived around here all my life. I'm a Wigan girl through and through!"

"That's great. I like having staff live near to the train stations," I politely remarked. I carried on.

"Wigan Girl hey?........Do you know Cath. Wigan is famous for two things?" I stated.

"Is pies one answer?" Answered Cath.

"No." I answered. "Beautiful ladies and Rugby league players ......What position do you play Cath?" I asked 😒.

The room went deadly quiet for a few seconds. Stevie G was gobsmacked. He looked round at me with glaring astonished eyes. The remark came as one hell of a shock to him. He soon got another 😲.

"Yer' not exactly George Clooney yourself', Baldy!" Cath replied.

Steve struggled to swallow.

I stood up.

"I've only got one thing to say to you missus!"

I walked around the table towards Cath. I could sense Steve shaking. I could sense his horror. Cath also stood up and walked towards me. Steve was now sh*****g himself 😱.

"Give us' a cuddle darling. You've got the job!"

Me and Cath had a right good hug 😍.

Steve was mesmerised. Totally confused.

He was so relieved when I explained all about Cath. He still remembers the knots in his stomach with worry that day. Even after this shock, Steve still says that was the best day's interviewing he ever did!

Yes, I did steal this joke off a Peter Kay comedy programme, but it was hilarious said in the right situation.

YOU COULDN'T WRITE IT 😂.

Cath the Wigan hooker! 😊

TAF

I'd like to introduce TAF (I will explain how he got this name later). In my fourteen years in Train Presentation Management, running the train cleaning for Northern Rail in the North West England area, I have come across hundreds of cleaners. I have interviewed hundreds of candidates. Honestly, I have managed some right thick b*****ds in my time!

One person in particular outshines, or should I say out-dulls, them all. He is way out on top of the 'Thicko' league. He is Champion's League Idiot Standard. There will be four stories involving TAF.

Having said that, it's all my own fault 😣. I interviewed him and took him on. There's only been a handful of cleaners I have regretted taking on. TAF was definitely one of them. It just goes to prove. You should not ALWAYS take on friends, or friends of friends from the pub.

Saying that, a nicer person you would never wish to meet. He wouldn't hurt a fly! He was a really nice guy. Good hearted, good timekeeper, good sickness record, smart in appearance, but honestly, thick as pig s**t!

I will start with his name.

He worked at Piccadilly train station for ten years. It was only when I was drunk on his retirement day, I told him why everybody knew him as TAF 😁.

When he first started, after 'passing' his interview, testing and training, (different stories to be explained later), he would mingle with the other cleaners at Piccadilly. He told stories of how his grandparents would take him to Rhyl or Prestatyn each year on caravan holidays.

TAF (I won't mention his actual name), was always convinced these holidays in Wales were the reason everybody called him TAF………Wrong! 😖.

All the cleaning and train staff, not just Northern Rail staff, but other train companies at Piccadilly as well, had got wind of his comical shenanigans during his interview, testing and training.

TAF did his first two weeks of on-the-job training. Basically, it wasn't rocket-science. All you had to do was get on a train with a plastic bag and litter pickers. Pick up the odd can, banana skin, newspaper or empty plastic coffee cup. Put them in the plastic bag and get off the train. The supervisor Harry decided to let TAF out on his own. What could possibly go wrong 🤷.

It was TAF's very first day on his own. Harry went looking for TAF because he was well late for his dinner break. He noticed some other train company cleaning staff laughing at the end of one of the platforms. They waved Harry over.

TAF was cleaning everybody else's trains! The cleaning staff at Virgin, Trans Pennine and the other companies were letting TAF clean their trains 😄. TAF was working his b*****ks off for them!

Harry had to laugh along with them, otherwise, he would have cried. Again, in hindsight, I suppose it was our own fault really. We should have told him that because he worked for Northern Trains, he should clean Northern Rail trains. Silly us! 🤷‍♂️🤷‍♂️.

It was this very day he got Christened TAF.

Getting back to his retirement day. Me and TAF had drank a skinful of beer. We were both p****d!

I should have just let sleeping-dogs lie, but I was very drunk. I told him how he actually got his name.

After that day of cleaning other company's trains, one old Northern veteran cleaner who had worked at Piccadilly for donkey's years had witnessed the whole comical farce. He removed his tobacco-less pipe. With his dry Northern humour, he simply said "TAF." 🤔.

"Pardon?" Someone asked.

"Thick As F**k!" He said. " TAF." 😄

From then on and for the whole ten years he worked at Northern, he was known as TAF. Hardly anyone ever knew his real name.

YOU COULDN'T WRITE IT 😄.

TAF'S INTERVIEW

I have to be perfectly honest. In life, we all make mistakes, naturally including me of course.

I knew TAF on and off for about fifteen years before he joined us at Northern Rail. Obviously, he wasn't called TAF then. It was more a case of letting on to him really, normally in the pub or bookies we both frequented.

Two mutual friends asked me to get ***** back in work. I heard he got sacked from his last job because he dropped a right clanger! I don't know whether it was a coincidence, but the factory he worked at burned down at the same time 😖.

Anyhow, getting back to the story. A train cleaner's vacancy came up at Piccadilly. I asked ***** if he was interested. Obviously, he was. I went through the normal procedure of advertising the job, sifting the candidates and arranging the interviews.

Prior to the interview date, I arranged and met up with ***** in a local pub. We sat in a quiet corner away from everybody. I went through all the questions I was going to ask him in a few days' time. The interview would be at our offices at Newton Heath. There were only ten or so questions. I went through the ten questions one by one. I told him the answers I would expect to receive back 👌.

"The one main thing *****." I emphasised to him. "When you get there, I will be dressed in a suit and tie. I will be with another manager and a lady from Personnel who will be taking notes. Honestly, he would have got confused if I would have said HR, Human resources. His brain only had the capacity for holding a very small amount of information 😮.

"The one main thing *****," I emphasised YET again. "The one main thing to remember. YOU DO NOT KNOW ME when we meet...... We've never met!"

I actually remember him saying. "I'm not stupid Keith. Mum's the word!". He meant to point to his nose, but accidentally poked himself in the eye 😣.

Yes, I know you can guess what's coming.

Interview day arrived. It was a Friday. ***** entered the interview room. He was very smartly-dressed.

I stood up and shook his hand. I remember his hand was sweating profusely, as was the rest of his body. It was a hot day. ***** had got there two hours early. He told me he didn't want to take a chance on being late.

As I said, he was dressed very smartly in a suit, waistcoat, jacket and overcoat. His face was red with beads of sweat on his forehead. I told him to take his overcoat and jacket off and to relax. He explained that he was ever so nervous. I asked him to take a seat.

"Don't be nervous *****. We don't bite!" I tried to calm him down. I gave him a secret cheeky friendly wink 😉.

As always, I started off with a friendly informal chat. As was normal, I asked him of his most recent job and if he was working at present.

Hindsight is a wonderful thing. I suppose I should have foreseen his response, but I didn't. More fool me!

"As you know Keith. I've been delivering bedding and pillows for them Asians from their factory at the back of your house!" Not only does he know my name, he also knows where I live 😖.

I stared in disbelief directly at TAF. I was physically stunned frozen into silence! Trying to restore my composure, I glanced my eyeballs from side to side. I didn't have to look properly. I could sense my two colleagues were looking directly at me. They both began chuckling 😃 😃.

I was sweating profusely now.

We somehow got through the interview, although I had to change his c**p answers. I later wrote down the answers he should have given us. He didn't answer one single answer to the point. In his anxiety and confusion, he wasactually giving out answers to different questions! 😨.

No word of a lie honestly. The other manager was a mate of mine thank God. He was convinced we were being pranked on a television show! He scoured the room after TAF's interview, looking for hidden cameras. He was expecting someone like Jeremy Beadle or Ant and Dec to walk in. He genuinely thought it was a set-up 😵.

We all make mistakes in our lifetime. This was definitely one of my biggest. I took him on.

As I have said from the start, ***** is a cracking bloke. But, from now on, I feel it is only fair to call him **TAF. (Thick As F**k** 😄).

There are more mistakes off TAF to follow.

YOU COULDN'T WRITE IT 😄.

TAF'S INTERVIEW! 😊

TAF'S TRAINING

After the debacle of TAF's interview, it was time for TAF's training.

Because the train cleaners sometimes had to work near the track, it was necessary for them to do a safety course. They had to pass the course test (PTS – Personal Track Safety). In my opinion, the course test was very hard, too hard for most new starters. So, with a little help from yours truly, the friendly instructors, and a little bit of cheating, most all the staff got through it. The PTS was not that vital to our train cleaners. They were never put in danger.

I'd just like to mention one little point before the test. TAF was an absolute nervous wreck at the thought of sitting any form of exam. I think his last test was written on a slate, sat next to Fred Flintstone. I gave him a few little pointers to learn before his course and test in a week's time. The main tip was to learn the phonetic alphabet. This came up in several questions. Obviously, TAF had no idea what I was on about 🫤.

"Alpha, Bravo, Charlie, "I said. "The police, fire and ambulance all use it. Certain people on the railway have to use it. You'll never have to use it, but you need to learn it for the test".

He phoned me up worrying. I told TAF to nip to his local library and get a book. It won't take long I told him. Just learn this bit and you are part way there.

Weekend came. There was no sign of TAF. Saturday and Sunday went by. Still no sign of TAF anywhere. He wasn't in the bookies or pub?

On the Monday morning one of the other cleaners Billy, phoned me up.

"What have you done with TAF Keith?"

"What are you on about?" I asked.

"I've just been speaking with his wife. He's hardly ate or slept all weekend. He's worried sick over his test." 🔲.

I called to his house. His wife Maggie, instructed me to go upstairs to see TAF. When I saw him, he was sweating. He was unshaven. He looked like a tortoise that hadn't slept for ages emerging from under his blanket 😖.

I soon got to the root of the problem. In short, TAF had been to the library and told the female librarian he desperately needed to get a book for a test for his new job. The only word he could remember was 'Alpha'. He had totally confused the librarian. He walked home with a book. The woman told him to play safe and take this thick in-depth book home. It covered everything TAF was warbling on about. She had given him the history and everything you need to know about Greece 😨.

He kept telling her it was an alphabet and it began with Alpha. Naturally, the librarian thought he meant Alpha, first letter of the Greek alphabet. The book was really heavy, about three inches thick! Poor TAF had been trying to read through the thick, (thick being the operative word!) book. He was reading all weekend without having a clue what he was looking for? Bless him 😄. I wrote the phonetic alphabet down for him and told him to learn this, but keep this paper on him just in case he needed to cheat.

On the first day of training, the instructor Mike, was his usual calm and pleasant self. He got his first taste of TAF just before dinner. The class of six had all been pre-warned to learn the phonetic alphabet. TAF had two full days at home to learn it. It's not that hard surely 🤷.

Mike went round the class and asked each one to spell their name phonetically. Colin was first. "Charlie, Oscar, Lima, India, November. C,O,L,I,N….. Colin."

"Excellent!" Mike commented." Billy, your go."

"Bravo, India, Lima, Lima, Yankee. B,I,L,L,Y…..Billy."

Three other new starters had their attempts…..All perfect!

Last but not least, it was TAF's turn. Mike and the rest of the class were stunned when TAF started his answer.

"G for George!" He said! (George is not his real name, but you get the idea). The rest of the class were in stitches laughing 🤣.

Anyway, back to the test. It was a two-and-a-half-day course with the test on the afternoon of the third day, the Friday. I purposely made sure TAF was sat next to someone who had some intelligence. I told TAF to look at the other bloke's answers, he wouldn't mind. I'd already had a word with the intelligent one. In other words. CHEAT! Just like other people do 😈.

TAF finished the test with thirty per cent. One of the lowest ever recorded scores in history. He was even too thick to cheat! Even with permission off his manager, me!

He only cheated on one question. The bloke sat next to him had written down "I don't know the answer to this one!"

TAF wrote "Neither do I!"

(Only kidding, I made that one up 😁).

TAF re-sat the test. He failed miserably again. He scored fifty per cent. The pass mark was eighty per cent. The normally placid instructor Mike was pulling his hair out by now especially after taking his next class of six to near the trackside for some on-site training. The idea was that when a train driver sees anyone near the track, he toots his loud horn. ALL workers then raise their hands to acknowledge the train driver.

Yes, you've probably guessed it again.

The driver sounds his horn. Mike and five trainees raise their arms. Thicko TAF doesn't! Mike was going apoplectic with rage 😲.

"Why didn't you raise your arm?" He screamed.

"What's the point? You six did, there was no need for me to do it as well. He MUST have seen us!" 😖.

I pleaded and persuaded Mike the trainer to give TAF one last chance. No pass this time, no job. Simple as that!

Desperate times lead to desperate measures.

In hindsight, it was me who was acting thick! I stupidly gave TAF all the correct answers on a piece of paper. In my defence, I wasn't thinking properly at the time. I think it was lack of sleep due to the worry TAF brought to the party. I was in charge of a hundred cleaners, but TAF drained me more than the other ninety-nine put together 😖.

I dropped yet another b*****k with TAF. I told him to get a few questions wrong. You WERE allowed twenty wrong answers after all.

Yes, you've guessed it again 😖.

The thick b*****d got every f*****g answer correct!.......NO ONE gets one hundred percent! Not even the top boffin managers!

He made me look a right idiot. It's all my own fault I know. I should have given him some wrong answers myself.

In the space of a week, it appeared that TAF had improved from a totally thick b*****d, to a f*****g genius! 😨.

YOU COULDN'T WRITE IT 😄.

TAF'S TRADING!

TAF GOES AWOL

Believe it or not, but not all trains arrive bang on time, all the time! Yes, sometimes they maybe a few minutes late! (Less of the sarcasm from me please).

At Piccadilly, the train cleaners have maybe five to ten minutes to litter pick the train before it departs again. If the train arrives a few minutes late and it takes a couple of minutes for the passengers to get off, it can leave very little time, if any, for cleaning.

On the rare occasion, the cleaner could get trapped on the train. The whistle would blow, the train doors would shut, and off goes the train with the cleaner on board. No panic, it happens. Get off at the next station and catch the next train back. Simple.

This normally happens once or twice to a cleaner in his career. This happened to TAF three times in a month!

The first time it happened was in TAF's second week on the job. Credit where it's due though. He had at least learned to clean our trains (Northern trains), and not the other company trains! (Sorry, sarcasm has crept in again 😖).

TAF was assigned to litter pick the Stoke train. Billy, his colleague got on the front of the train, TAF got on the back. The idea being to meet in the middle. Billy warned TAF that there were only a few minutes before the train would set off again.

So do what you could in a couple of minutes, then get off 'el rapido'.

Billy got off when he heard the whistle, the train doors shut. TAF was nowhere to be seen on the platform. Billy looked through the windows of the departing train. Through one window, near the rear of the train, he saw the sweating panicking TAF sprawled across a passenger table banging on the window 😮. There were shocked passengers sat around the table watching the embarrassing spectacle.

Billy stood in slow motion, shaking his head watching the sprawled, panicking stranded TAF slowly pass by. Once he had finished laughing his b*****ks off, Billy went to inform his team leader Harry. Once Harry had finished laughing his b*****ks off, he contacted Railway control. Once Railway control had stopped laughing their b*****ks off, they contacted the guard on the Stoke train. They told the guard to pass a calming message on to the panicking cleaner.

"Don't panic, these things happen. No harm done. Get off at the station and make your way back to Piccadilly."

An hour later. No sign of TAF?

Two hours later, there was still no sign of TAF? Harry was now getting very curious and concerned.

Three hours later, TAF is spotted on the station by Billy. He was walking down the platform towards the concourse. Billy asked TAF what had happened. TAF filled him in. Billy could not wait to tell team leader Harry what had happened. Billy made his way to the cleaner's office.

"I'm glad you're sat down boss. I have a little story for you." Billy couldn't wait to tell the story.

"I've just been talking to TAF. He reckons it's your fault he's late!"

"My f*****g fault!" Shouts out Harry 😨.

"You told him not to panic and get off at the station."

"Yes, that's right. Stockport. It's only ten minutes away for God's sake?"

"No. You told TAF to get off at THE STATION! He took that station as being Stoke. Because he was on the Stoke train, he thought you meant Stoke."

Billy was now uncontrollably laughing in stitches. Harry's face had turned red in anger 😤.

"He's been gone over three f*****g hours!" Harry was wound up alright! "Come on, I need a fag!"

Harry and Billy went outside, they both smoked. As they lit up, Harry repeated himself again in frustration.

"Three f*****g hours, I just cannot believe it!" 😰. He sounded like a wound up Victor Meldrew.

Billy broke out laughing again. Harry was shaking his head in disbelief.

"What's so hard to understand?.......What's so hard to understand Billy?......Stockport is just down the road. He could've been there and back in half an hour?"

Harry now looked like the police inspector Herbert Lom played in the Pink Panther. Steam coming from his nose 😤.

Billy was still uncontrollably laughing away 😄.

"Three f*****g hours! What's so hard to understand?" Harry carried on with his rant. "He's only been here for a fortnight. He's doing my f*****g head in! There are ten stations between here and Stoke! Has he not got half a brain cell telling him to get off at ANY ONE of them, for Christ's sake?.......Thick b*****d !" 😨.

The more Harry ranted on, the more Billy fell about laughing. It wasn't long before Harry broke down laughing as well 😂 😂.

They spotted TAF walking towards the mess room with a brown paper bag in his hand. He was merrily whistling away like he didn't have a care in the world 😗.

"What the f*** is he doing now?" Ranted Harry.

"Oh, I forgot to tell you boss. He's just been in Sainsbury's and Greggs. He's off for his dinner hour now!" 😄.

Harry was in total disbelief mode now. "Give us' another one of your fags Billy , for God's sake!"

Harry had been diagnosed with high blood pressure. He had given up smoking before TAF joined Northern. He now smoked double the amount he used to! 😨.

I think it is fair to say. Harry developed at least a dozen more grey hairs in TAF's first two weeks at Piccadilly. Although Harry was in his late fifties, I used to tell people he was only thirty. It was all the worry with TAF that aged him so much 😖.

YOU COULDN'T WRITE IT 😄.

TAF GOES AWOL! 🙂

Northern Trains

THE REALLY FIT CANDIDATE

I was interviewing for a vacant train cleaner position at Buxton train station. As always, I had a responsible relevant colleague interviewing with me. In this particular case it was Liz.

Liz was the train cleaning team leader at Buxton. She was a cracking girl, (no doubt she still is!). She worked nights cleaning trains at Buxton for five years before being deservedly promoted to being a guard. Buxton has its own weather system up there, I'm telling you. It could be fine in Manchester but could be under a foot of snow up there 🥶. It was that bad at times, even the trains couldn't get through.

Whatever the weather, Liz would brave it through. Despite the regular awful weather conditions, Liz was always upbeat. She was down to earth with a great sense of humour. She never moaned, she just did the job and got stuck in.

Anyway, getting back to the story.

Six candidates had been sifted and selected for interview. Liz and myself met early at Buxton train station for a coffee and to discuss our plan of attack for the day.

We interviewed four of the candidates before taking a well-earned half hour lunch break. Liz had a walk round to clear her head. I did some paperwork. As always, I phoned my beautiful partner Mary 😍.

Liz as expected, got involved, speaking with all the candidates. As I said previously, Liz was down to earth with a great sense of humour. She was being her natural self.

A few minutes before we interviewed our penultimate candidate, I explained to Liz that I had received a phone call from our HR (Personnel) Manager. We had to interview an extra candidate added on at the end. I told Liz that this was most unusual. It had never happened before. Apparently, the late entry was a relative or a very 'good friend' of the Chairman of Northern rail 🫤. I told Liz that I didn't even know if the 'good friend', was male or female.

We interviewed the last two official candidates. It was time for our 'special guest' late entry. I asked Liz if she could go and collect our mystery guest who should be in the booking office waiting room.

Liz came back to the interview room. She politely knocked on the door. I looked up to see Liz enter the room. She was excitedly raising and dropping her eyebrows, rocking her head forwards, sideways and backwards! I knew she was warning me of someone special following her in 🫤.

"Keith, this is Marianna".

Marianna entered the room. I could see why Liz was so excited 😀. Marianna was a stunner! She was immaculately dressed in nice shoes, nice tights, a cracking tight-fitting dress, with a stylish jacket top. She was so pretty and had a body to die for! She smelt gorgeous as well.

"Marianna, this is the manager, Keith".

I stood and shook hands with Marianna. Liz came to my side of the table. She was still furiously moving her eyebrows up and down at me! Marianna took her jacket off, revealing her cracking figure 🤩.

We began with a convivial introductory friendly chat. I must admit, I began flirting a little from the very start. Very unprofessional of me I know.

"Before I start the interview, Marianna. Can I just say you smell and look gorgeous!"

Liz looked worriedly sideways at me. I raised my eyebrows in return at Liz. I was not acting in a totally professional manner.

"Have you had any cleaning experience Marianna?" I asked.

Marianna continued to give perfectly acceptable answers. As she did so, I leant to one side of the table and began looking down at Marianna's legs. Liz was getting ever so nervous 😰.

I began to ask another question but hesitated half way through.

"Please forgive me Marianna. I cannot take my eyes off your legs or boobs! They are absolutely perfect!"

Liz heavily smashed her knee against mine.

"Well thank you," replied Marianna.

I stood up and walked behind Marianna. Liz was now becoming a quivering, nervous wreck 😦.

As I stood behind Marianna. I bent over her smelling her hair. Liz's eyes could not possibly have gotten any wider! She had literally now changed colour to a ghostly white, whilst heavily sweating. She was in shock. On the verge of a breakdown, I recall.

I put my hands just below Marianna's breasts and kissed her neck. Liz was frozen, sweating profusely 😦.

"I only have one more question Marianna. Sleep with me tonight and the job is yours?"

"Agreed." She answered.

I could not carry it on anymore. Liz was on the verge of having a heart attack or a nervous breakdown 😰.

"Liz, I have spoken to you loads of times about my partner Mary. This is not Marianna. This is my Mary 🤩.

We could feel the pant of air in relief from the other side of the table!

"You b*****d!" Liz dropped her head into her hands on the table. She raised her head…… "You awful b*****d!"

"You planned this all along you b*****d!" 👿.

In her defence, normally Liz hardly ever swore.

"No, I phoned Mary at dinner time. Mary thought it would be a good idea to have a couple of drinks in Buxton and a meal on the way home. I hatched my devious plan there and then!" I explained.

I must admit, I was always up to pranks. I still am.

Twenty minutes later, Liz had recovered! Her heartbeat had returned to normal. She was now laughing and joking with Mary. They were good mates now. It took quite a while longer for ME to get back in her good books though.

We all had a few drinks and a cracking laugh about the incident in the local Wetherspoons. Liz and Mary literally made me pay for my prank. They ordered very large expensive gin cocktails 😠.

YOU COULDN'T WRITE IT 😄.

PONGO

I would like to introduce PONGO. He was without doubt the most irritating, scruffiest person I have ever come across. He smoked like a trooper, at least sixty a day. He drank like a fish, at least ten pints every day 😨.

He was argumentative about everything. He was extremely rude to people. He had no respect for anyone, especially women. He didn't give a t**s what people thought about him, his body odour or appearance. Surprisingly, he never married.

He looked like a cross between Claude Greengrass off Heartbeat and Uncle Albert off Only Fools and Horses. He stunk like an overflowing ashtray on a heavily beer-stained table. I hope you are getting some sort of picture of Pongo.

He was always involved in trouble at Newton Heath, arguing with everyone. He was warned several times about his appearance. Because he worked nights away from customers, plus the fact that his union rep was just behind him in the 'scruffy league', somehow, he always got away it 🤷.

He got breathalysed twice at work, but miraculously was under the limit on both occasions. Pongo always had a few tricks up his sleeve. He always carried three two pence pieces with him. In his locker, he would have a bottle of vinegar and a packet of Fishermen's Friends lozenges. If he found out he was going to be tested, he would put the two pence pieces in his mouth and suck on them. He would then get the vinegar, spit the coins out and swill his mouth with vinegar a few times 😒.

Finally, he would shove half a dozen Fishermen's Friends in his gob. For those that don't know. One Fishermen's Friend lozenge is hot and strong enough 🥵.

Eventually, things came to a head with Pongo at Newton Heath. He was even discussed at a director level meeting.

As luck would have it (or bad luck for me, as it turned out), a vacancy appeared at Buxton. The station is in the middle of nowhere. It is the thoroughly ventilated with howling winds blowing through it normally. The job was cleaning trains throughout the night with not another person in sight. The only things he could upset there, were the odd rat, fox or lost sheep. Perfect place to put Pongo.

I was summonsed to our Manchester headquarters where upon I was 'politely asked' to accommodate Pongo at Buxton. In other words, Pongo WAS going to Buxton, out of the way. I had no say in the matter 🤷.

A meeting was arranged at Newton Heath. This was another sickening but funny story in itself.

In attendance from the management side were myself and Joanne, the Personnel Manager. Joanne was marvellous at her job. She was always immaculately, eloquently dressed and turned out. She was so professional, well-spoken and extremely feminine. Yes, Joanne was intelligent, posh and gorgeous 🥰.

Into the office walked two scruffy, smelly b*****ds 🤢. To make things worse, it was the middle of summer, we were experiencing a heatwave. Pongo and his union rep, Pongo two, sat facing us. Joanne was in for one hell of a culture shock I'm telling you. I introduced everyone. I shook hands with the two scruffs, so did Joanne.

My hand felt slimy and greasy. It smelled of engine oil or something similar. I could see both Joanne's hands were physically shaking. I did not know whether to laugh or cry. I remember recalling a thought of Mrs Bouquet dipping her hand into a bucket of cow dung 😒.

Just as the scruffs moved backwards to sit down, one of them farted loudly 🤢. To this day, I don't know which one of them 'let go'! All I do know, is that neither of them batted an eyelid. This was just normal behaviour to them. They were both so uncouth!

The smell hit you immediately! I can still remember Joanne turning her head ninety degrees to look at me. Her nose and ears were visibly twitching, like she was instantly allergic to the air. I could see her eyes begin to water behind her glasses. I felt so sorry for Joanne but I did fully warn her she was in for a shock ☐.

The room smelled of tobacco, bad eggs and body odour. Sat in front of us were the Dirty, smelly, Hairy Cleaners! They were like two hillbilly lookalikes of Claude Greengrass and Jim Royle!

The union rep (Jim Royle look-a-like), was scruffy enough, but trust me, Pongo was in a league of his own 😠.

He had at least two thermal vests on, a Northern polo shirt, a jacket plus a thick hi- viz overcoat. He probably had a few pairs of thermal socks on as well. The smell of sweaty feet was now mixed into the room's fragrant aroma 😖. I turned the hot radiators off (I swear someone turned them on intentionally). I opened as many windows as I could for ventilation. Jim Royle wore his fair share of clothing as well. Neither of them took anything off in the sauna like room.

The two had met up together in a transport café just over the road in the High Street in Newton Heath Centre. It was obvious they had eaten a full English breakfast each. Pongo had a collage of food colouring around his scruffy greying beard. Brown sauce, red sauce, yellow egg yolk. He even had an orange baked bean still lodged in there 😕.

Occasionally, you could see a dew drop slowly develop under his nose. It was OK though. Pongo would readily wipe it away on his sleeve cuff 😮.

His partner in crime wasn't so bad really. He only had a banjo down his shirt. For those that don't know, a banjo is the yellow yolk of an egg stained down his shirt front. You hold one arm out with the egg butty in, whilst wiping the spilt egg yolk off the belly with the other hand. It looks like you are playing the banjo. It's easier explained face to face.

We started our meeting. I looked over at Pongo. I couldn't take my eye off the lone baked bean nestled in his beard, with heavy brown sauce stains either side of his mouth. He had spots and a rash either side of his nose under his eyes. Both eyes were bloodshot with a white crisp coating around his eye lashes ☐.

Not surprisingly, the meeting was one of the quickest either Joanne or myself had ever been involved in. Pongo was very keen on the idea of moving to Buxton, plus his excellent terms and conditions. No other people or bosses would be there during his night shifts, except poor old me occasionally 😕.

His union rep ensured he got all the extra benefits. Three hours extra travelling time every day, supervisor's rate, working alone extra rate, loads of overtime working six or seven nights every week. Pongo would be rolling in money. All his birthdays had come at once.

As the scruffs left the room, it might have been my imagination, but I'm sure one of them let rip again 😖. Joanne rushed out to the ladies. She must have vomited. Her eyes were red and watery when she came out ten minutes later.

This story is an introduction to Pongo. Believe me, there is more to come!

YOU COULDN'T WRITE IT 😕.

Pongo is dressed, for a meeting!

PONGO HAS A SHOWER

I picked up Pongo and drove him the more or less exact marathon distance of just over twenty-six miles to Buxton. As was mostly the case in Buxton, it was a freezing cold night. However, I drove all the way with two car windows open. I was freezing my b*****ks off, but this was the better option. Pongo stunk to high heavens, plus he lit up a fag every five minutes 😖.

I took him up to Buxton to give him an induction of the train station, show him the ropes. I showed him where trains would be parked, water supplies, toilets, mess room, stores, fire evacuation points etc. I instructed him on all the necessary health and safety aspects of Buxton train station.

He instantly fell in love with the place. He was in his element. He was in the middle of nowhere. No bosses hounding him, no people to upset. There was nobody knocking about all through the night. He was generally, permanently on his lonesome. He'd see the odd train driver last thing at night and first thing in the morning. He'd see the odd drunk sleeping on a bench. He'd see foxes and rats at night, but his smell kept them away! Pongo had fallen on his feet 😀.

He got to find out that Steve, one of the conductors, had recently split up with his girlfriend. She had been caught s******g a married train driver on one of the trains. Steve was desperate to take in a lodger in order to pay towards the rent and bills. Enter Pongo onto the scene 😧.

They were like the odd couple. However, the arrangement suited them both. Steve was always clean and smartly dressed. Pongo was just an uncouth, smelly, scruffy b*****d! They hardly met. Steve worked through the day and slept at night. Pongo did the opposite. Pongo was on a winner. He was getting travelling time every day, there and back because he was based in Manchester. He worked six or seven nights every week. He was on supervisor's rate, he got extra for working alone. He was loaded! What could possibly go wrong 🤷.

In his first three months I received several complaints about Pongo, all coming from the Regional Train Manager, Don. It's fair to say they were not on each other's Christmas card list. Pongo was accused of smoking in the mess room (not allowed). Sweeping all the train dirt and rubbish onto the tracks (not allowed). Sleeping half the night on a warm train (not allowed). Sleeping half the night in the warm mess room whilst leaving the porn channel on the large fifty four inch tele' turned on (not allowed). Urinating off the platform onto the track (not allowed). Thank God there were no cameras there at the time.

I visited him several times at Buxton, approaching the accusations. Every single one was denied. The train staff had complained of the mess room smell every morning. It stunk of farts, body odour and cigarette smoke 😫. They took photographs of burnt-out cigarettes left on a table. Some of the fags had two inches of ash still stood on the end of the cigs! He still denied it was him! Pongo had now become an official fire hazard at Buxton. Some of the staff, both male and female, complained that each morning the television was left on showing the same lesbian porn channel when they came in work to watch the BBC breakfast news on tele'.

All these matters were addressed. Pongo somewhat adhered to my warnings. He was given several written warnings. Even his equally smelly union rep, Jim Royle lookalike was happy with my decisions. Pongo knew he couldn't spoil such a good thing. He knew where his bread was buttered alright.

Another couple of minor Pongo complaints riled the Regional Train Manager. His hair was turning greyer by the week since Pongo arrived 🥵. Although I got on great with Don, the Regional Manager, I was accused of favouritism and not taking the appropriate action against Pongo.

One day I got an informal anonymous tip off. A secret clandestine night visit to Buxton had been arranged. It was to be a few days later on the Thursday night of that week. Don, The Regional Manager was calling with an independent union rep and a female Personnel Manager.

Early on the Thursday morning, I 'coincidentally' called to do a train clean audit at Buxton. Obviously, this was not the main reason for my visit, but killing two birds with one stone and all that. I checked and knew that conductor Steve, Pongo's landlord, was working that morning. When I got to Buxton, I asked Steve for a private quiet word.

Confidentially, I told Steve of the secret visit that night. I told him that it was in everyone's interest if Pongo did not mess this up. For one night only, Pongo had to make a determined effort starting with his appearance and his personal hygiene. Steve agreed to make sure Pongo had a good shower Spray on lots of anti-perspirant. Shave or trim his scruffy grey beard and put on clean uniform. It wasn't his birthday. This was far more important 😣.

I'd finished my audits by eleven. I knew exactly where Pongo would be. He would be on his fourth pint in Wetherspoons at the bottom of the hill near the station. He had the same routine more or less every day. Finish work for six in the morning. Walk to the newsagents to buy the Sun newspaper, (mainly for the boobs on page three), and forty fags. He would walk to a bench near the Pavilion Gardens. Crack open a can of beer he'd found on a train that night or previously. Light up a cigarette, then begin reading the paper always starting at page three!

At around seven he would go for a full English. The café owner would pass him each morning. They would open up the shop together. Pongo would have his breakfast, three massive mugs of tea whilst picking his horses. He would visit the bookies for half an hour before making his way to a local pub which let him in the back door hours before official opening time. He would time it right to reach Wetherspoons for their opening time.

Anyway, I met up with Pongo in Wetherspoons. He bought me a pint. He should do as well. He was on more money than me with all his perks. I explained to him that his 'best mate' Don, the Regional Manager was coming down that night or early morning. I explained the importance of giving a good clean performance. I told Pongo I had also told Steve. This was because the chances were that Pongo wouldn't remember after getting p****d, as he did every day 😠.

Nine o'clock that night, I get a phone call off Steve.

"You won't believe this Keith!"

'For f**k's sake. What's Pongo done now'. I distinctly remember thinking this 😖.

Steve carried on. "I was on the phone to work before. I had already told Pongo he had to have a shower and smarten himself up. Whilst I was writing my roster hours down, I was keeping an eye out watching Pongo. The bathroom door was partly open so I could sort of make out what was happening."

I closed my eyes worrying what was coming next 😖. "Go on." I said worriedly.

"As usual Pongo had fallen asleep on his bed still wearing all his smelly uniform. I woke him up telling him he had to shower and smarten himself up. He woke up and walked into the bathroom. I saw him take off his jacket. Then his pullover and shirt. He took off two thermal vests throwing them all to the floor. He took of two pairs of thick thermal socks with massive holes in them. Then his soiled (inside and outside), trousers. He threw some underpants onto the floor. I could see from my chair the underpants had all sorts of different coloured stains on them." 🤢 . Steve swallowed heavily.

"He came to the bathroom door starkers. Jesus Keith, what a sight! Can I use your shampoo he asked. I was still on the phone, I nodded. He gets in the shower. I hear a shout when the water is turn on. I'm still on the phone talking to work. Ten seconds later, the shower is turned off. He starts drying himself. I could clearly see him. Honest Keith, the bottom half of his body was bone dry! The water did not get past his huge beer belly or fat a**e." 🤢 .

"Unbelievable!" I said to Steve.

"I've not finished yet Keith!"

My eyes closed tightly again in horror anticipation 🤢 .

"He only puts on the same stinking heavily stained undies! The same two pairs of stinking holy sweaty socks! The same smelly thermal vests, shirt and jumper! I got a stinking whiff off his work pants as he put them back on." 🤢 .

"Dirty B*****d!" I groaned.

"Next thing I know Keith, I hear the front door shut. He's gone off to work an hour early. When he does that, he usually calls at Wetherspoons for a couple before he starts!"

"I give up!" I moaned 🙅.

YOU COULDN'T WRITE IT □.

Pongo has ten second shower! 😖

PONGO AND THE OTHER TRAMP

Pongo remained at Buxton. The scenario ticked a lot of boxes really. It suited him, it suited us. He was alone throughout the night in the middle of nowhere in Buxton. His appearance, body odour or argumentative nature became less of a fear factor there 😊.

Steve the conductor was getting half of all his bills paid by Pongo who was staying at his house, although Steve's air freshener bill went up quite a bit.

The one thing you couldn't fault Pongo with, is that he ALWAYS turned up for work. Unbelievably, he was never late or sick?

It would be extremely difficult for me to get someone else there at the drop of a hat. This was a vital factor for me in the Buxton equation.

The complaints about Pongo slowed down, although they still trickled in now and again. The Buxton train drivers and conductors somehow took to the enigmatic Pongo 😦. He would do the drivers a favour by starting the trains up at four o'clock in the morning in preparation for the morning checks which had to be done every single morning by the designated driver on duty that day. This would give the driver an extra hour in bed. Yes, it was totally illegal and slightly dangerous, but blind eyes were turned now and again at Buxton ▯.

One bloke who detested Pongo was the Peak District Area Train and Station Manager Don. He was very high up in the Northern structure. Don was also a highly respected magistrate and school governor in the Peak district area. His wife was a governess and MP. He was a man to keep on the right side of. Talk about chalk and cheese with him and Pongo! All the complaints about Pongo came from him via his train and station staff. I had at least a dozen email complaints off Don about Pongo 🙁.

Don and myself arranged secret unannounced audits. We would visit Buxton about four o'clock in the morning. Nobody knew we were coming. I tell a lie! It definitely wasn't in my best interest to have poor audit results plus drop Pongo in the s**t. Pongo couldn't afford to have bad audits as well. Don would have sacked Pongo on the spot if he found out Pongo had started a train up. Don would have cherished this 😃.

I would always tell Pongo we were coming. He in turn would tell the designated train preparation driver, who would then turn up early, on time, to do his train preparation job properly. It was only once a month!

Pongo would make an extra special effort on our 'secret' early morning audit visits. One of his many tricks was to buy half a dozen air fresheners from the pound shop in Buxton. It would only cost him a few quid! There were normally six trains to clean each night. He would use a full can of fragrant air freshener on each train! Although Pongo was a right scruffy b*****d, he was a devious right scruffy b*****d!

Even Don thought Pongo was improving 😮.

Getting to the story at hand.

About five o'clock one weekday morning, I was awoken by a phone call. I wasn't best pleased! It was Don phoning from HIS bed. He wasn't best pleased either!

"Keith, I've just had an irate call from our Independent Train Audit Inspector at Buxton!" Yelled Don! "He says there is a f*****g tramp on the first train due out!"

I must say at this point, Don was an educated posh well-to-do bloke who very rarely swore.

I gave him the obvious response.

"Tell him, it's a Northern employee. Tell him, it's scruffy Pongo!"

"Of course, I f*****g told him that!" Screamed Don 😤. He didn't need a phone. If I had opened my bedroom window, I could have heard him scream from Derbyshire from my house in Denton!

"Pongo is stood next to the f*****g tramp! He was smoking a f*****g cigarette along with the tramp. They've just got off a f*****g train together! 😤."

Don had used up his normal year's supply of swear words in less than a minute 😖.

I arranged to drive up to Buxton early that morning.

It was just after eleven o'clock when I got there. I asked a few questions at the station before walking down the road to the Wetherspoons in Buxton. I knew exactly where Pongo would be.

On entering Wetherspoons, I immediately spotted (and smelled) the two scruffy b*****ds sat at a table in the far corner drinking beer.

'If you can't beat them, join 'em!'

I bought myself a pint of lager and walked over to join them.

"Alright Keith, this is my mate Lazlo. Lazlo, this is my gaffer, Keith."

I shook hands with Lazlo. To be honest, he was probably cleaner than Pongo. It turns out Lazlo was Polish. He'd fallen on hard times after breaking up with his Russian wife! He spoke excellent English, actually, better than Pongo.

The three of us spoke for a good twenty minutes. Pongo definitely avoided talking about Lazlo cleaning the trains. I brought the matter up.

It turns out, Pongo had spotted Lazlo walking around the centre of Buxton a few times. He ended up buying Lazlo a soup and a pasty from Greggs. The following day, Pongo spotted Lazlo walking past another pub in the centre of Buxton. He buys him a pint and gives him a couple of fags. He more or less gave Lazlo his own unofficial job interview in the pub 😖.

The rest is history as they say!

For the past two weeks, Lazlo had been turning up at the train station at night. He'd been cleaning most of the trains! Picking up litter, mopping all the floors, replenishing the toiletries, everything! Both Lazlo and Pongo had thought all their birthdays had come at once!

Lazlo was glad to get stuck in.

Pongo would spend half the night asleep after drinking a few cans, watching lesbian porno films on the big screen television in the staff mess room, w*****g himself silly to sleep every night. I'm sorry. It is crude, but it's true! He even used to admit and boast about it 😯.

I had already caught him asleep a couple of times when I visited Buxton in the very early hours of the morning. He was snoring away. He had left the tele' on. It was always on the lesbian porn channel! I told him that I had forgotten to mention to him that the Buxton Area Train Manager Don had hidden CCTV installed in the mess room last week. Honestly, it's the only time I ever saw Pongo sweat □.

I carried on the charade for another hour. Poor Pongo was s******g himself! I couldn't carry it on any longer. As I was leaving, I told him that I was joking about the CCTV cameras!

You should have seen the relief on his face, it was a sight to treasure 😃.

It turns out, Pongo had three large lockers in the changing room in the station. He had left them open the day I called up. Jesus! It was like an Aladdin's cave in that locker room! He had loads of cans of beer, bottles of wine, packets of crisps as well as other drinks and foodstuff in one locker 😠.

In another locker, he had some watches, mobile phones, lighters, jewellery etc. In the third he had an array of umbrellas, clothing and other bric-a-brac! Everything that had been left on the Buxton trains were in there 😯.

Lazlo would bring in found goods every morning. Pongo would pay Lazlo in already found cans of beer from his bank. Found cigarettes and found foodstuffs! In other words, Lazlo was working his b*****ks off throughout the night and getting paid with part of the stuff he had already handed in. Pongo was earning a fortune for doing f**k all except w*****g himself to sleep and collecting all these free goodies 😦.

YOU COULDN'T WRITE IT 🤐.

PONGO AND THE TRAMP! 🙂

I SPY

I remember many moons ago taking my two children Stacey and David down to Beswick to visit my Mam. Mam would have (still has), toys for the kids to play with keeping them amused. David was about four, Stacey was about six. David was beginning to learn letters and spelling words. We decided to play a game of 'I spy'. As always with siblings, everything was a contest. They were both desperate to get one over on each other, even at this early age arguing like cat and dog 😖.

Stacey had her go. "I spy with my little eye, something beginning with P (obviously pronounced puh)". After a few guesses we eventually we got it. Picture!

Mam had her go (K, pronounced kicking kuh). We got it...Keys. I had my go C (curly kuh). They got it. Carpet David and Stacey would shout their guesses out, desperately trying to get the correct answer first.

It came to David's turn......"I spy with my little eye, something beginning with.........M (muh)".

"Mirror ?" Shouts Stacey......."No!" Replies David.

"Monkey," I guessed. (There WAS a monkey on a book, by the way). "No!" David smugly replies 😊.

"Mother?" Tries my Mam......"

No!" Replies David

We tried looking around the room. We tried a couple of other obscure guesses, but there literally wasn't anything else beginning with M. The three of us were completely flummoxed 🙀🙀🙀.

"We give in," I conceded.

"It's dead easy. It's right in front of you all Silly Billys!"

We looked in front………Still no idea?

"Come on David, we give in!" Said Mam. We were all getting a little agitated by now.

"It's dead easy!.......'Mote control for the tele!" He answered! 😠😠😠.

Funnily enough, we didn't get David's second selection either when he chose double L (luh, luh). I won't bore you with our guesses, but his answer was 'Lectric Lamp! 😯.

YOU COULDN'T WRITE IT 🤭.

STAMPEDE AT THE BACON FACTORY

Throughout my working life I only ever had two main jobs. The first, straight from school, was with British Gas. Most of my twenty odd years there were spent as a manager. The other main job was performing as a train cleaning manager with Northern Rail Trains. I spent fifteen happy years there.

Anyway, getting to the story. In between my two main jobs, I worked at Ashton foods (in Ashton, Greater Manchester, believe it or not). The factory produced a wide variety of bacon products, employing hundreds of local people.

All employees had to wear the required health and safety clothing whilst working on the shop floor. Everyone had to wear a builder's type safety helmet, a hair net and ear plugs, a buttoned-up, white butchers-like coat, amongst other things. Worst of all we had to wear these thick cumbersome bright yellow wellies 😣. You were embarrassed to wear them at first, but you got used to it. Everyone had their own personal locker in either the ladies or gent's locker rooms.

There were a couple of cracking yellow wellie pranks I soon picked up.

There was always a large gap at the top of everyone's wellies. At a certain part of each production line, there was a metal vessel which caught the sharp corner edges of the plastic bacon packets. These were small sharp triangular or star shaped plastic cut offs. The trick was to grab a handful, walk behind your target before emptying the sharp bits into the big gap at the top of their wellies. It was normally done with an accomplice who would distract them by keep the target talking.

It was slightly evil, but hilarious to watch 😈. Within seconds of the target walking away, they would shriek and start limping in pain 😖. The small sharp plastic clippings would bite into the feet. They would be very quickly emptied out from the wellies. I got done on my very first morning!

The other wellie prank was more basic, but just as funny.

You would simply walk past a fellow worker. Everybody at first would fall for it.

You would simply say. "Be careful mate/love, your laces are undone!" Then carry on walking.

You would be amazed how many people stopped, then bent or looked down at their lace-less wellies 😃.

Another amusing prank we did was blowing up the blue disposable plastic gloves. Certain workers on the line had to wear these gloves when touching the bacon. We'd blow them up then tie a knot in the bottom bit which kept the 'hand balloon' inflated. We made different designs. One or two fingers sticking up, maybe was the most common. All you had to do was stick the other fingers down to the plastic glove with sticky tape. A bit more sticky-tape was formed into a circular shape. The sticky-side on the outside of course was then stuck onto the glove.

As I mentioned before, everyone had to wear builder's type safety helmet. It was an absolute doddle to simply place the one fingered inflated glove for example, onto the back of the helmet. The target couldn't feel a thing, but would walk around the factory unknowingly sticking the finger up at everyone. Course, nobody would tell the victim. It was childish but dead funny 😆.

It broke the day up. Nobody (workers, supervisors, managers), were exempt from the prank. Although I invented the prank, I got caught a few times myself 😖.

Bosses would be the only people who would remove the offensive shaped, but hilarious inflated plastic glove balloons. The secret was not to get caught sticking the balloons on in the first place. Sometimes, you would get half a dozen people walking around the factory floor at the same time unintentionally sticking their fingers up at the happy workers 😃.

Other designs were later invented such as windmills, flowers, flags etc. These were stuck on helmets as well.

The victim always felt embarrassed when they found out, but trust me, it was so funny 😄. Some took it worse than others!

Anyway, getting to the story (at last I hear you say! I feel like Ronnie Corbett sometimes, telling one of his lengthened rocking-chair jokes).

This was partly illegal and naughty, but funny nonetheless.

As I said before, everyone had their own personal locker. I am not saying Tameside is a den of iniquity, but a fair number of packets of bacon found their way into people's lockers 😈. Different people had their own method of walking off the shop floor with bacon. Bringing the bacon home if you like.

My mate Chris was a Quality Control Inspector. His method was easy. He would simply take a pack of bacon, openly rest it on his clipboard and blatantly walk off the factory floor with it. No one would suspect, he could have been checking the bacon for anything. There were multiple different checks required. Quality, weight, labels etc. He would walk straight to his locker. He had it away with about four packs a day. (They won't know it's you Chris 😊).

Others used to stash packets of bacon down their wellies or inside their trousers at belt level, front or back! Other people had their own personal plans.

My method, (I mean a friend of mine's method), was to place a pack under my (I mean his) armpit, walking out holding my (I mean his), finger with the other hand pretending the finger was hurt. This gave me (I mean him), a firm grip on the bacon under the arm. Everything was covered by the large loose white coat. I (I mean he), would pretend to wander off to the toilet to rinse my (I mean his), finger under cold water. I (I mean he), would then off load the bacon into my (I mean his), locker! 😈.

One day a female worker went absolutely berserk. She had gone into the work's canteen for dinner. She had left her handbag on the table. A few minutes later, on her way back to the shop floor, she realised she had left her handbag in the canteen. She was mortified 😖. Her bag contained her passport, flight tickets and holiday spending money 😰. She was staying at her sister's house that night, before flying out to Benidorm first thing the following morning for their annual family holiday.

She 'flew' back to the canteen. The handbag wasn't on the same table.

She went screaming into the top manager's office. She was frantic and inconsolable with worry 😦.

Management decided to carry out an immediate full scale locker search. This would be carried out instantly by management, a union representative, the woman herself along with the individual person who used the particular locker.

Here's the funny bit 😃.

It was just after dinner. An urgent announcement came over the factory Tannoy system.

"A very valuable piece of property has gone missing from a table in the canteen. A handbag containing a passport, money and holiday tickets has gone missing."

All the machines were turned off. The factory fell silent.

"There will be a full impromptu supervised locker search carried out with immediate effect."

Honest to God. It was like a comedy sketch 😨.

There was literary a stampede of workers rushing out of the factory shop floor exit door. All rushing to somehow empty their stash of bacon from their lockers!

I (I mean my mate), nearly got squashed in the rush of about twenty stampeding bodies.

Ironically, the search was called off almost immediately. The woman who had 'lost' her handbag forgot she had given it to her sister for safe keeping 😦. Her sister had taken the handbag home for safe keeping as she was on a half day working.

It was hilarious talking about it in the pub later, but at the time it was scary! I, (I mean my mate), nearly s**t myself (I mean himself) in the rush 😀.

YOU COULDN'T WRITE IT 🤯.

CLEAR AS MUD

Last year I drove my mate Colin to a private eye hospital in Didsbury, South Manchester. (I'm always doing him favours 🙇). He's not posh or rich, the eye hospital was one of many getting rid of some of the massive backlog of basic cataract operations from the over loaded, over worked National Health Service.

We parked up at the eye hospital just off Princess Road before signing in at reception. We headed straight for the free coffee machine before taking a seat in the large spacious reception waiting room. There was probably another thirty people sat waiting. Each patient had to be accompanied by someone else as an escort. When the simple procedure had been completed the hospital insisted the patients got away safely.

In the waiting room, one elderly extrovert gentleman stole the limelight. He stood out from everyone else. He never stopped talking 😦. He was in his late seventies, eccentric and very smartly dressed. He wore brown and white brightly patterned shiny leather shoes that resembled tap dancing shoes or something out of an old gangster movie. He wore stand out bright orange and yellow tartan checked trousers with a matching waistcoat. He wore a nice brown tweed jacket with a similar coloured matching dickie bow. Topping his attire was a smart brown trilby hat with a red feather attached on the side. He was definitely colour coordinated alright.

He was only five foot tall with what looked like darkened tinted spectacles. Me and Colin instantly nicknamed him Ronnie Corbett 😊.

We sat a solid hour listening to his stories. He was very loud for such a small man. It turns out he had been an entertainer on the entertainment circuit many years ago. He then became an undertaker working close by in South Manchester. He still helped out at the undertaker to that day. He joked how busy he was with the covid epidemic. You couldn't help but listen to him. You had no choice really 😄.

Every so often, patient's names would get called out. They would leave the room soon to be replaced by new patients. Ronnie Corbett would regularly go to reception complaining of his waiting time. He would then walk the short distance to the front door to smoke on a massive cigar outside. Talk about smoking stunting the growth. I swear, he looked smaller every time he walked back in. He'd come back in and immediately start another one-way conversation with the same sorry lady patient who took the brunt of him ☐.

Apparently, his daughter had left him there. The plan was for him to ring her once he was ready as she had business very close by. She was no fool. I'm sure I spotted a woman matching her appearance in a cafe at the small roundabout before you reached the hospital 😃.

Half an hour later, Ronnie Corbett was getting really p****d off. He went ranting to the young Asian male receptionist causing a right fuss. According to 'Ronnie', he'd been waiting three hours 🤢. His appointment the week before had been cancelled at short notice, another two had been cancelled for whatever reasons and a fire alarm had stopped another appointment! He frequently moaned of how he was supposed to get round if he could barely see 🥴. He complained of how badly his eyesight had deteriorated over the past six months.

His moaning may have worked. His name was called out. The whole waiting room breathed a sigh of relief. He wasn't that bad really, he made most of us chuckle.

Ten minutes later Ronnie Corbett returned to the waiting room. His seat was still empty. He reached into his jacket inside pocket, pulling out his very small antique Nokia phone. He is then clearly heard telling his daughter that he was ready to get picked up. This confused us all a little bit 💁.

Ronnie sat forward. He pushed his trilby hat upwards, letting out an audible sigh. He turned to the lady sat next to him. She'd just had two hours of him.

"That's it then." He said shrugging his shoulders.

"Have you been sorted already?" She asked.

"Yeh, the doctor sussed it straight away. The doctor explained the sudden worsening of my eyes. It's simple, I'm sorted now."

"That great news!" Compliments the woman.

We are all listening intently now.

"The doctor took my glasses off and raised them up to the light. He got a little blob of cotton wool, dipped it in surgical spirit and wiped my glasses. There you go, Bob's me' uncle!......I'm cured!"

Half the waiting room were shaking their heads, the other half were chuckling away 😄. His glasses weren't tinted after all.

"He reckons it's all that dust and s**t working in the crematorium the past six months. Along with my cigar smoke, it's covered my glasses in s**t!" 😄 😄.

YOU COULDN'T WRITE IT 😄.

As clear as mud! 🙂

CHAT! CHAT! CHAT!

♫ I can see clearly now ♫

THE ANGRY CHEF

It started off a normal peaceful Bank Holiday Monday. It was early dinner time at the Village Hotel, Hyde, Tameside. I was sat in the bar area with my best mate Colin, (most unusual I hear you say). Colin brought his beautiful wife Julie with him. I had been drinking in the bar for a good hour before Julie and Colin came in. I'd knocked back three pints already. We were off having an afternoon out in Uppermill.

In this hour, I witnessed the young barmaid Kate running around like a blue a***d fly 😖. She was ultra busy. Kate was on her own. For some reason, the Village was woefully understaffed that day. Poor Kate was pulling her hair out and getting stressed doing as much as she could 😧. Being a sunny bank holiday, lots of people, mainly families, were coming in for drinks and pub lunches. Add to all this, the rostered chef had not turned in for work.

The supervisor Rebecca called at the bar to assist. She also got stressed as well trying to sort other things out as well as help Kate at the same time. Rebecca frantically phoned around for staff, especially a chef. Meanwhile, Kate was informing the long queue of customers Chef was on his way. Meals would be available soon.

Marcel, the excellent Cuban chef, was the standby chef. First reserve if you like. He couldn't say no really. He was recently given a written warning □.

Marcel had just worked ten straight days on the bounce. On the day before, the Sunday tea time and evening, he celebrated his short break from work on the 'Razzle!'. Deservedly Marcel got bladdered along with some friends. Beer, shorts, shots, you name it, Marcel knocked them back 😆.

He's a 'Rum Dude' when he's out of work celebrating, is our Marcel, I'm telling you! However, people were humoured that the chef was on his way, nearly there. They had no idea how hung over he was though 😖.

Kate and Rebecca continued to fight the flames, keep those plates spinning. Enter Marcel! He is popular with staff and customers. We, all the regulars, let out a loud cheer and clapped our hands. Marcel raised a middle finger towards our table 😃.

He was suffering from one monster of a hangover. His eyes were like bloodshot p**s holes in the snow with dark heavy rings around them. He looked more like Uncle Fester out of the Adams family. He hadn't had time to shave, his hair was dishevelled. He looked and must have felt like a wreck 😠.

He went to the staff room to put on his chef's clothing. He returned to his kitchen. Nothing had been prepared whatsoever. Pans could be heard smashing to the ground. Marcel was not a happy chappie 😠.

"What the f**k!......What the f**k!" Could be heard coming through the serving hatch. It wasn't funny......I tell a lie. It was hilarious! Every smash was met by a loud cheer. Our table were laughing our heads off 😄.

In hindsight this was not a good idea. Marcel is a big bloke. He has been known to throw big carving knives as a party trick. Add to this he was furious, hung over and stressed rotten. Rebecca told us to shut up. Do not antagonise Marcel. He was close to the edge 😖.

Marcel snatched a long list of food orders stuck to the serving hatch top. Rebecca went into the kitchen offering help and trying to calm Marcel down. She ran back to the bar where another queue had formed. She hurriedly walked past us shaking her head in frustration. Tension was rife 😰.

Burgers along with chicken wings or tenders with chips are the most popular orders. For some reason, buffalo chicken wings were highly popular that day. Marcel stormed out of the kitchen heading towards Rebecca and Kate busily serving at the bar.

"There's a' no chicken wings!!!...There's a' no chicken wings for f***s sake 😖. I am a' cooking the chips, but there is a' no chicken wings!" Marcel was on a right rant. Honestly, Marcel does not usually swear as much as that.

At this point, I must give Julie full credit for the story ending. I thought it was an absolute cracker 😃. She knew things were heated (or not as the case was). She nudged me saying something quietly in my ear.

"Keith……He's frying without wings!"……..What a cracker! Brilliant! I just could not resist! I started our rendition of Westlife's Flying Without Wings! I changed ONE letter only.

"He's FRYING Without Wings. He's FRYING Without Wings!" 😄😄.

All the regular customers, plus new customers picked up on it straight away and joined in. It was hilarious 🤣🤣🤣.

Even more so when Marcel popped his head through the serving hatch raising his middle finger at us again.

"Keith……Why don't a' you go and a' f**k a' yourself!"

A big cheer went out yet again 😄.

Days later, Me, Colin and Marcel had a great laugh over the absolutely true bank holiday rant. We still do!

Once again, full credit to Julie for the gag, and Marcel for taking it so well😄 😄.

YOU COULDN'T WRITE IT 🤣.

OH CAROL, I AM SUCH A FOOL

Me and my best mate Big Col', often visit our local Village Hotel in Hyde, Greater Manchester. Probably three weekdays every week. We are both members. We frequently use the sauna and steam room facilities. We ALWAYS use the bar facilities after (Don't tell Julie. She thinks Colin spends all his time in the pool, sauna and the steam room 😃 😃).

Amongst our many friends at the gym are Carol and Lyndsey. We invent nicknames for all our friends and staff there. It's our little private funny hobby. Colin, to Lyndsey and Carol's great annoyance nicknamed them **** Ladies! (Lyndsey and Carol know the name, nobody else does). I told Colin this was an awful nickname. We dare not call them that name anymore. Lyndsey would bite our heads off 🥴. They are two good looking, smart, decent ladies, with good senses of humour.

Lyndsey is a very good-looking young lady in her early thirties. Carol is a good-looking lady in her mid-seventies. Carol can still do the splits and get her leg onto the four foot plus high bar! She is not much taller herself!

Carol is a little naiver than Lyndsey. She has fallen for a few of our pranks. I once told her they had removed the word gullible from the dictionary. She believed me! Only joking Carol, I made that one up. Them two together, and we as a group, are very good friends.

Every time we meet, we have a laugh. The girls are often in stitches 😄. Sometimes though, it does not go plain sailing. A joke may not go down well.

As mentioned previously, Colin mainly, and myself play tricks on the girls. Lyndsey has bitten my head off a few times 🥴. Carol just the once! Sometimes I may go a little too far I admit. It's me that does the pranks mainly, not Colin.

The one-time Carol did fall out with me, was after I created an April Fool's prank that didn't go down too well.

On the Thursday prior to April Fool's Day (Saturday, only last year 2023), the four of us were talking in the bar area. We were talking about April Fool's pranks we'd played in our younger days.

May I just mention at this juncture, the ladies don't drink alcohol, although Colin and myself have been known to sample the odd half 😊.

Lyndsey and Carol both mentioned that nobody does April Fools anymore, Besides, they would NEVER fall for one!!!

Cue me. That gave me something to aim for. I went home that day thinking of what devious plan I could muster. That same night, I had concocted my plan.

The plan was to tell the girls I needed a massive favour doing on the Saturday morning (April Fool's Day 2023). I needed one of them to phone me up and get me out of a tight corner. I would tell them I had to take my Auntie out shopping. This (made up), was a nightmare because my Auntie always wanted to go everywhere, calling to at least ten different places. This would normally take hours 😖. Lyndsey and Carol both know how much I like my early Saturday drinking session around the pubs of Denton. The favour I would ask was to pretend to be my new girlfriend and phone me up when my Auntie would be in the car with me listening on the speaker. Basically, that was the backbone of my plan. I told Colin of my plot.

On the Friday afternoon I walked into the bar room. Lyndsey and Carol were sat in their usual places having a coffee and a corned beef butty each. Carol (although not allowed really), always makes corned beef butties and eats them in the Village, the little devil!

I purposely placed my coat on a chair near to where the girls were sat. I ordered the beer. With my pint, I sat on a high chair at a table about three yards from the girls. This was our normal places to sit. I noticed Colin approach the bar entrance which was situated behind the girls. They could not see him. I nodded my head to him. This was the signal for the start of our plan. Colin phoned my mobile telephone number.

I pretended to watch the sport on one of the large screen televisions as I normally do. I heard my phone ringing in my coat pocket but purposely ignored it. I heard Lyndsey call at me, but pretended to be interested in the sport on the tele'. Carol and Lyndsey both yelled at me "Keith. Your phone's ringing!" 😗.

"Oh, sorry girls, I was miles away." I answered in my brilliant acting manner, as I walked towards the girl's table. I picked my phone out of my coat pocket. I answered it. Colin said "OK?"

"Yes," I replied.

Colin finished his call. Half of his work was now done.

I talked on my phone. Obviously, there was nobody on the other end, but the girls did not know this 😖.

"Hello Auntie, how are you?"

"Yes, I am….." I continued my charade. I paused another few seconds, making it all sound plausible.

"I can Auntie, but I need to be back home for eleven o'clock. I'm taking my new girlfriend out for the day."

I paused again.

"Yes Auntie, she is very nice." I carried on purposely blagging in front of Lyndsey and Carol.

"She is Auntie. Yes, very pretty!" I winked at Lyndsey 😉. The girls were very interested now.

"Yes, she's gorgeous. She's a nurse." I winked at Lyndsey again 😉. Lyndsey and Carol were sat open mouthed and wide eyed with interest now.

"She has been on nights all week. She deserves a nice break. She is going to phone me in the morning when she gets up. So, I will pick you up about ten o'clock. Is that alright Auntie?" I said a few more words before hanging up.

"What was all that about? Everything alright?" Asked Lyndsey. Colin now entered the room heading for the bar.

I explained to the girls that my uncle had gone to an away game watching Manchester City. My Auntie needed to go shopping. My Auntie had asked me to take her. The problem is, she takes absolutely ages going around different places 😖.

I now needed a massive favour! I needed one of the girls to phone me in the morning and pretend to be my new girlfriend. The plan would be for my new girlfriend to ask if she could be picked up ASAP. We were to enjoy a day out in Sheffield at the snooker and the shopping centre. My Auntie would be listening to this on the speaker phone in the car. It was crucial that the phone call would have to be made very soon after ten when I had just picked her up. She would be sat in the car listening to the conversation.

I told the girls I didn't mind taking my Auntie shopping, first thing, but I had to get back early to meet the lads in the usual pubs in Denton. It was the law on a Saturday morning. It was my ritual, sacrosanct! 😀.

"No problem, I'll do it!" Offered Lyndsey. "What exactly do you want me to do?"

"Phone me just after ten. It had to be this time. I will have my phone on the car speaker. You pretend to be in love with me.

Give it all the 'Lovey Dovey' stuff 😉. Say you want picking up from here (The Village Hotel, Hyde), as soon as possible. Say you are looking forward to sleeping with me again. Simple!"

"I'm not being 'Lovey Dovey' with you!" Said Lyndsey 🙁.

"She doesn't KNOW you. She'll never ever see you. It's all an act!" I persuaded her.

The second part of Colin's involvement was now about to kick in. I had earlier given him a piece of paper with the telephone number of a friend of ours who goes in the Village with us. Gareth is very quiet and shy. He was going through a hard time with his missus. They were always falling out.

I knew it wouldn't take long. I had been waiting.

"I need your telephone number Silly!" Said Lyndsey.

"Of course! How stupid am I!" 😗.

I searched for a pen. Enter Colin's second role in the plan.

"Here. I've got a pen!" Colin said.

"Write my number down please Colin." I winked at him 😉.

Colin did not have a pen but pretended to write a telephone number down. He walked over with Gareth's mobile telephone number already written on piece of paper, handing it over to Lyndsey. The plan was working to perfection. If I say so myself, our acting had been near Oscar standard 😀.

Soon after Carol and Lyndsey got up to leave.

"Change of plan," said Lyndsey. "I might have to go out in the morning. Carol's phoning you instead."

"No problem! Great! Cheers Carol. Don't forget. Just after ten. Don't let me down!"

Carol raised her thumb. "I won't let you down Keith, promise. Don't worry."

The girls left. Me and Colin started laughing our b*****ks off. The plan was going to perfection 😄.

"You'll get us shot!" Laughed Colin. "There's no turning back now, they've left."

"Don't worry. It's only a joke!" I said.

What made it even more amusing, quiet unsuspecting Gareth then walked in 😯. He knew nothing of the prank. He asked what we were laughing at. We told him it was a personal joke.

Saturday, April Fool's Day came and went. I heard nothing. Monday, Tuesday, nothing 😕. Wednesday dinner, I met up with Colin in the bar in the Village.

"Carol's going to rip your head off. She's fuming!" 😳.

"What's up?" I asked sheepishly.

Lyndsey then walked into the bar area alone.

"You've done it this time Keith. Carol is devastated! She's not stopped crying for three days! She's not slept for three nights ☐. She's getting ready downstairs (in the gym changing rooms).

Honestly Keith. Your name is mud!". Lyndsey went back down to console Carol.

Again, you could not plan the timing so good! Shy Gareth walked in. He got a pint and sat with me and Colin. Ten minutes passed, Gareth as ever, hardly said a word 🤐.

"Did you get a phone call Saturday morning Gareth?" I asked.

"I most certainly did!" He answered.

Gareth is a little nervy at the best of times. He carried on.

"I was driving the missus and kids to Wales. Just after ten o'clock this woman comes on the phone." Colin noticeably sat back taking a big swig of his beer. I was getting nervous myself now.

"She says Hiya' gorgeous, missing you to bits! Can you come and pick me up from the Village? Can't wait to sleep with you again later! The missus went f*****g berserk! 🥴. I asked the woman who she was. She rang off! The missus was giving me daggers! Five minutes later the woman phones me again. I kept saying you've got the wrong number love. Neither the woman herself or Diane (Gareth's missus) were having any of it. Then the woman says 'that IS Keith from the Village, isn't it?'

It was only then I cottoned on! I tried to explain to Diane that it was just Keith doing an April Fool's prank like he does! We were half way to Wales. We argued that much, we ended up turning back. Me and Diane have now split up 😕. She didn't speak to me all day. She hasn't spoken since 🤐. The kids have been crying. It's been a f*****g nightmare!" Gareth rarely swears by the way!

Me and Colin were now nervously swigging heavily on our pints. In walks Lyndsey.

"You'd better go in there and talk to Carol. She's in tears." 😭.

I walked into the reception area with Lyndsey. I sat with Carol on one of the hotel couches. She WAS in tears. She said she'd been crying and worried sick because she'd let me down. She'd phoned my number but could not get her message across properly. She had been worried ever since that she had totally let me down 😭.

She said she had been up all Friday night, practising her lines. Different ways she was going to be Lovey Dovey to me. She even locked herself in a room at ten to ten in the morning because she did not want to be disturbed or distracted by anyone until after the important phone call 😯.

I felt I had no other option other than to come clean. I walked into the bar dragging Gareth back with me. Colin followed. What started as a joke had turned into a disaster. I think the only two people that found it funny were Colin and Lyndsey. Colin because I took all the flak. Lyndsey because the prank could have quite easily been played on her had she not changed plans last minute 😂 🤣.

I told Carol it was all meant to be a joke. April fools!

"I heard your phone ring. I heard you speaking to your Auntie. I even saw Colin write your number down?"

"Sorry Carol. It was all planned by me."

"Who did I call then?"

I looked round and nodded at Gareth 😖.

"He dropped me right in the s**t with my missus as well, Carol!"

"Colin phoned me from the door over there. I was then speaking to nobody. I wrote Gareth's number down earlier that morning in my house. Sorry Carol...Sorry Gareth." 😒 😒.

It took a bit of time, but eventually everyone has forgiven me now......for the time being at least. They have all promised to get me back. I think I will disappear abroad on April the first this year 😠.

YOU COULDN'T WRITE IT 😅.

CAROL'S PLAICE

We have a good laugh in the bar area of the Village hotel in Hyde, Tameside. There's never any trouble, just good-natured banter. There are regulars in our friendly gang who sit with me and Colin. Ladies first. Lyndsey, Carol and Christine, then Stewart, Dom and Gareth to name a few. (Just thought I would throw a few name-checks in, they might buy the book if they're in it!) 🤣. This is another one for Carol.

One Friday dinner, several of us were sat on high chairs around a couple of tables. Carol had to be lifted onto hers, she only has short legs 😊. As usual, we were having a right good laugh. The beer was flowing. Well, it was for me and Colin at least. As usual, jokes were flying around left right and centre. We were all in good form. Other guests and bar staff would pass our table and join in the laughs.

Around the table this particular day, were Lyndsey, Carol, Christine, Stewart, Gareth, me and Colin. Question time!

Colin asked. "What's the biggest Country in the world?"

We all had guesses, (I obviously knew the answer, this is one of our trademark joke questions. A few of the others, especially the men, knew as well). The normal sensible answers came in. China, Russia, Greenland, Australia, Canada? Colin answered NO to them all. In the end we all gave in.

"Ireland!" Came the correct answer from Colin. This confused a few of our gathering, most especially Carol 😟.

"I've been to Ireland," she said. "It can't be!"

"It is! Trust me." Insisted Colin.

Things went a little bit quiet for a few seconds. You could see it playing on Carol and Lyndsey's minds. Carol would not have it. She was confused. After a minute or so, I decided to put Carol out of her misery.

"Come on Colin. It cannot possibly be Ireland surely." I said in my pretend fake voice. "Why's it Ireland then?"

Colin answered. "Because it keeps 'DUBLIN' all the time!" 🤣🤣.

A cheer went around the table. Most of us were in on the joke. Carol sat pan-faced, still confused. Lyndsey leant over and whispered in her mate Carol's ear. It took a short while for the penny to drop before Carol burst out laughing.

"Stupid sods!" She yelled at us. "I should have known better. You silly sods!" 😠.

We bided our time for a while. We threw some serious simple questions in as decoys I raised yet another of our trademark joke questions. Again, most of us knew it was a joke. Lyndsey and Carol didn't know.

"Name three fish that start and finish with the same letter?"

"Ah good one," came a fake pretend comment.

"Trout!" Shouted Lyndsey with glee!

"Well-done Lyndsey. Two to go." I congratulated.

A minute later, Clever-Clogs Christine piped up. "Turbot!"

"Excellent Christine! Only one to get now."

I looked over at Lyndsey and Carol. I could picture the cog wheels going around in their brains, desperate to get the last fish.

"What does it begin with?" Asked Lyndsey, hunting for a clue.

"K," I said. "It finishes with K as well Carol!"

"I knoor, I knoor. I'm not stupid yoor knoor!" She snapped again, (only jokingly), in her broad Ashton accent.

"I knoor yoor knoor." I replied. I like to take the mickey out her accent. It gets on Carol's nerves 😊. I can't talk or call accents. My accent is the broadest Mancunian.

"Oh p***s off you silly sod!" Carol retorted 😠.

After a minute or so, I stopped their pain.

"Kilmarnock is the answer!" I shouted out.

It took a few seconds before Carol reacted. She stood up on the side struts of her high chair.

"Kilmarnock?....That's a place!" She screamed out.

The rest of us let out another loud cheer!

"Correct Carol. It's a PLAICE!!!" 😊

Her face turned red as she was stood up outstandingly alone on her high chair. She still had her index finger raised, pointing upwards. She very quickly sat down resting her forehead on her arms on the table. She slowly started shaking her head in her arms.

"I don't knoor why I ever listen to you silly sods. I really 'doorn't'!" 😁 .

She had a good laugh about it soon after......She is a good laugh, is our Carol 🤭 .

YOU COULDN'T WRITE IT 🤭 .

Carol's Plaice! 🙂

FOR DUCK'S SAKE

Quite some years back, my best mate Big Col and his wife Julie visited Chelford Farmer's Market. For those that don't know, Chelford is a small market town near Macclesfield, noted for its superb farmer's market. You can buy absolutely anything farm related from Chelford.

Walking around the market Julie and Colin bought various things. Fresh eggs, plants, vegetables, salads, beef, pork, lamb etc. They passed an enclosure containing live ducks. Each time they got near the ducks, Julie would excitedly stop to look. She was drawn to one duck in particular.

"Let's get a duck Colin." 😃.

"Don't be silly Julie" Or words to that effect came the reply😠.

They walked around a bit longer. Julie kept mithering Colin to buy the duck. Despite Colin's objections, as ever Julie got her own way 😃. They actually bought a live duck! Julie had christened the duck even before they got it back to the car. Colin carried 'Dozy' the duck back to the car in a large box. It had to be large, the duck was heavy and massive. They were told Dozy was a Welsh Harlequin variety of duck. Colin was also warned by the farmer, that these ducks could be vicious. Their natural method of attack was to bite at the b*****ks of the human male species□□.

As soon as they got back home, Dozy was let loose to roam free in their back garden in Tameside. The garden was securely fenced off all around. Colin and Julie very soon found out that ducks s**t a hell of a lot 😣. Within hours, there was duck poo everywhere around the garden. This problem had to be addressed 😠.

Directly across the road from their house is a patch of barren land owned by the Church Council. Colin bought a dog lead. He would regularly march Dozy across the road for an hour or so. (This must have been a sight in itself 😊). Dozy would s**t all over the place in there as well. Colin reckons Dozy had a poo at least thirty times a day 😦.

Dozy would continually soil their garden. It became a full-time job for Julie cleaning the duck muck up all the time 😣. They were advised by some experts to get a duck pond installed in the garden. Colin knew everyone round Ashton and Stalybridge (well everyone in the pubs anyway 😀). Dave was one such person. Dave had installed dozens of duck ponds.

The ground foundation was dug out. The stone pond was fitted with all the correct linings and materials. Dave had done a great job. Colin was informed that the pond now needed to have a pump and filtration system fitted. This would dilute duck poo and keep the water fresh which was the whole idea. Dave advised Colin to get the Hozelock 3000KT filtration unit. This was the best and most reliable system. He wrote the details down. Dave insisted on Colin getting the Hozelock 3000KT filtration unit.

Colin decided to phone around getting prices and availability. Believe it or not, there weren't too many duck pond filtration unit specialist suppliers in Tameside. After several phone calls, Colin struck lucky (or not, as it turned out). He found a company in Congleton who specialised in these matters. What's more, he spoke to a bloke who knew absolutely everything about ponds, pumps, filtration units, acidity levels, temperature control, duck shit! You name it he knew it! What this bloke didn't know was not worth knowing. Obviously, he was so boring and irritating to boot. He was a pond Geek alright 🤓.

Colin began the telephone conversation in a very polite manner.

"Good morning. I'm enquiring about the price and availability of a pond pump and filtration unit, and if you have one in stock, please."

"Yes sir. May I enquire the purpose of your enquiry?"

"Yes, all I need is a Hozelock 3000KT filtration unit please."

"Certainly sir. But for what purpose may I ask?"

"I've built a duck pond in my garden. I've been told to put a Hozelock 3000KT filtration in it."

"With all due respect sir. One cannot install any old unit, Willy Nilly. I've been in this business over thirty years. Right sir, just a few questions if you don't mind."

Colin was started to get wound up already. All he wanted was a yes or no on availability and the price of the Hozelock 3000KT filtration system! 😠.

"You say for ducks sir? How many ducks?.........Is your garden North or South facing sir?...... What area of the country do you live in sir?..... Is there much vegetation close by sir?......Do you have problems with birds, mice, rats, insects, wildlife or any other pest's sir?" 🤓.

"Only you at the moment!" Colin answered 😠.

"No need for sarcasm sir. I'm only here to help."

"Have you got a bleedin' Hozelock 3000KT unit or not!!!!"

"If a job's is worth doing, it's worth doing proper sir. Now is your pond stone lined sir?....How deep is the pond sir?.....Will you be keeping fish in the pond sir? If so which species sir?"

"Is a duck a f*****g fish mate? Is there such a thing as a Duckfish? Do they quack quack swim! It's just for a s******g duck for Christ's sake!!"

"Calm down sir. I'm putting your details into my filtration calculator. I cannot abide impatience or sarcasm sir." 🤓.

A few pressing of computer buttons could be heard down the phone.

"Ah no sir. We don't have the Hozelock 3000KT in stock, but I can send you information on more intricate but slightly more expensive units. Now, what town do you live in sir?"

"Dukinfield." Answers Colin.

"I warned you about sarcasm sir!" 😳.

He hung up!

YOU COULDN'T WRITE IT ⚡.

LYING LITTLE TOSS POT

A Train Presentation Team leader's position (cleaning supervisor), became available at Piccadilly. I sifted through the applicants, whittling the list of twenty candidates down to six for an interview. One of the six applicants was a good friend of mine. Let's put it this way, Harry stood a good chance!

Joking apart, Harry was perfect for the job. He had all the right attributes. He was good with people. An experienced supervisor elsewhere. Excellent timekeeper, reliable and so on. Harry already worked four years as a train cleaner. He ticked all the right boxes.

However, being the professional I am 😇. If there was genuinely a better person at the interviews, they would get the position. There wasn't. I gave Harry the promotion. There was no favouritism, he genuinely deserved it.

During the interview with Harry at Piccadilly train station, platform ten interview offices, I noticed a familiar name on his list of references. A mutual friend of ours, Brian Robson. No, not the famous footballer, Captain Marvel of Manchester United and England fame, but a small business owner from Denton, Manchester, where we all live.

I say small business owner because Brian is, well, very small 😀. He reckons he's possibly five feet tall? He is more the size of a Milky Bar Kid or captain of a Subbuteo team captain.

Harry, quite rudely in my opinion, nicknamed Brian Little Toss Pot! Hence, a little clue to the title of the story. Anyway, less of the small talk. Sorry for any little puns on Brian 😉.

Brian owned his own heating and ventilation company, so he was a good point of reference for Harry. I must admit, I did not contact many referees if any! I left this to others. In this case I made an exception. I jotted down Brian's mobile telephone number. I could feel a prank coming on. I admit, I do the odd one!

After the day's interviewing and when Harry had finished his days work at Piccadilly, I drove us both back to Tameside for a celebratory pint. We arrived at one of our favourite watering holes, the White Gates in Hyde. We looked through the pub window to notice Little Toss Pot, I mean Brian, sat down inside. He was sat alone at a table with a full pint and a short (there I go again!) 😀.

Harry and myself went through the side entrance into the back room of the pub. Let the fun begin! We sat in a far corner. We could see him through the glass of a door. He didn't see us.

I must say at this juncture, that Harry likes a pint or two! That's putting it mildly! Do you get it? MILDLY? He still does, I'm telling you!

He was single at the time. He drank like a fish, smoked like a chimney, swore like a trooper and gambled like Maverick! He was one of the lads alright! He worked hard, he played hard. We had some great times.

I called Brian's mobile telephone from the back room. Harry was sat by my side. Brian didn't have my number, he did not know who was calling. I put on a strange Yorkshire accent. I don't know why, it just did?

"Hello. Is that Mister Brian Dobson?" Yes, I said Dobson wrongly on purpose.

"Robson." He answered. "Brian Robson. Like the famous footballer." He boasted.

"Oh sorry. My name is Phillip Robinson, Personnel Manager Northern Trains."

My mate Phil Robinson was actually the Depot Manager at Newton Heath. He is a good mate of mine. I was meeting him later that day. It was an easy name to remember in case the sly old fox Brian Robson tried to catch me out. I was normally pretty thorough with my pranks though.

"I am phoning you with regards to a reference you provided for a Mister...er...er Harry...er Bredbury." Another deliberate mistake on my part. Harry's surname is Bradbury 😊.

"Bradbury!" Answers Brian.

"That's what I said. Bredbury."

"No. It's Bradbury!" shouts Brian. He's already getting wound up 😠.

"Well let's agree to disagree." I said, being as awkward as I could. "I think it's Bredbury." I continued.

We could see from the other room. Brian raised his arms in frustration 😠.

I continued. "The decision on whether Mister Bredbury gets the job or not is literally on a knife edge. It could go either way depending on your answers."

The barmaid is stood in between the two rooms of the pub. She knew our prank. She could see and hear everything from the middle. She began to laugh her t*ts off 😄.

"I am a devout Christian. I deplore any form of vice. I see them all as sins. As a human weakness if you like. Does Mister Bredbury drink any sort of alcohol at all?" I asked.

"Nah. He never touches a drop." Comes back the lying answer 😖.

"Does Mister Bredbury smoke at all? I cannot abide people who smoke. An evil vice. A sign of the devil!"

"Never!" Answers Brian whilst blowing out a huge cloud of smoke from his massive big fat cigar. The cigar was not far off the same size as him 😂. "He's called Bradbury!" Maintained Brian.

"I will decide what he is called if you don't mind!" I carried on acting awkwardly. It became surprisingly easy.

"Does Mister Bredbury blaspheme or gamble in any form?....To the best of your knowledge, has Mr Bredbury ever sinned?"

"Never!" 😖. Came another lie.

"Are all your answers absolutely true? May God strike you down." I asked.

"Of course they are."

Me and Harry stood up with our pints and walked to the door dividing the two rooms. The barmaid was loving this 😄.

"Last question sir. In general, does Mister Bredbury lead a good moral upstanding life? Not fornicating with women of ill repute?" I asked.

"No way," answers Brian. "He's virtually a saint."

We burst through the door. In unison as planned, we yelled out.

"You lying little Toss Pot! You lying b*****d!" 😀😀.

Still holding his phone in one hand and massive cigar in the other, Brian sat back in shock. His little legs dangling from the bench.

"You pair of f*****g wankers!" 🫣.

We all had a right good laugh about it and still do. We got LLTP (Little Lying Toss Pot) a pint...not a short! 😀.

YOU COULDN'T WRITE IT 😄.

MAD MICK DOES BEST MAN

Mad Mick is one of my best mates. He has been for over thirty years. He's not mad, but he has done some crazy things in the past. He is a character! He has never harmed anyone in his life.

He once walked in the snooker club in Hyde, went to the toilet, completely stripped off except for a pair of hob-nailed boots. He folded his work clothes up neatly, placing them on a chair. Starkers, he walked nonchalantly to the bar and ordered himself a pint of bitter.

The trouble was, nobody was surprised at Mick's antics, least of all Kelle working behind the bar. Kelle didn't bat an eyelid. She served Mick, gave him his change and served the next customer 😲.

The following week Mick and his dearly beloved brother Lee. (God rest his soul!), did the same thing together in the club. I wasn't there but apparently Lee won the improvised manhood size competition (if you know what I mean), hands down 😀.

Mick is a great lad. He can normally smoke a fag in a minute and drink a pint in ten. This is his normal behaviour. He can go through a lot of fags and beer in a four- or five-hour session, I can tell you. If there was an Olympic event for drinking and smoking, Mick's our man! I would put him in the sprint, middle distance and marathon events. Guaranteed gold medal winner!

Saying that, you could not wish to meet a nicer person. He's a great laugh. He would help anyone out. 'Life's for living', is his motto. There will be a few yarns involving Mick in other books👌.

Anyway, getting to the story at hand. Mick was best man at his best mate and brother Lee's wedding. RIP Lee. He was also a cracking bloke! Lee was getting married at the Village Hotel in Hyde, Greater Manchester. Lee and Mick had each bought smart matching light grey suits. Big mistake. Schoolboy error. Especially for Mick!😖. The two brothers walked in Wetherspoons in Hyde. Dutch courage was called for before the wedding.

I was sat in Wetherspoons with my son, our David. There was a gang of about a dozen of us in there. As soon as we clocked Lee and Mick, the obvious loud wolf whistles and cheers went up 😃😃. They had tried to keep the wedding secret from us. They looked really smart in their light grey suits, dickie bows and carnations pinned to their jackets. It was only half ten on a summer Saturday morning. Lee wasn't getting married until one. Still time to back out I hear you say!

Mick as he always does, quickly started knocking the pints back. Lee would sensibly miss a round or have a short instead of a pint. A few whiskeys had calmed Lee down, He was a bag of nerves when he walked in the pub.

After an hour, Mick had knocked four pints back. He asked me if there were any pubs near the Village Hotel, the wedding venue. I told him there was a nice bar in the Village Hotel itself. I suggested Lee should spend his last hour of freedom in there with us. Ideal really, same place as the wedding! I was, and still am, a member there so could get a decent discount off the beer prices. It was decided. The Village Hotel it was 👌. That was our next and final watering hole before the wedding. We called a taxi. Hardly surprising, me and Mick were both desperately bursting for a wee.

As we were both 'relieving' ourselves in the Gents, Mick turned sideways looking at me. "Hey Keith. Have you seen this?"

It was a sight I will never forget as long as I live. Mick turned his body to face me. He raised both his arms in the air. He was still peeing. I couldn't help but look down. Absolute truth this, honest. There were three jets of wee spraying in different directions. Honestly, one to the right, one to the left, the other straight forward. All three sprays of wee shooting upwards 🙁.

"What the f**k?" I know I shouldn't have been, but I was mesmerised at the sight of his water flow exhibition 🙁.

"I can't explain it. One of them things in life mate." I remember him nonchalantly saying. Mick doesn't give a toss. Thinking about toss, I wonder if Mick's sperm……No I won't go there 😖. He must have done some things right. He has six kids, two girls and four lads! Anyway, some people nicknamed Mad Mick 'Three Ways' after that scene. (We have a local DIY store in Denton called Three Ways) 😀.

I finished my wee, obviously Mick had more fluid to empty, even though he had three outlets 🤪. I went outside in the sun to wait with Lee and our David for the taxi. I remember it was a beautiful summer's day. Shortly after Mick came out of the pub. He held both hands to his belly. He turned round pointing his bum at us. He let out the loudest fart! He was oblivious to his appearance. He turned back round to face us. He had a massive dark wet patch around his right-hand-side groin area!

This really stood out on his nice light grey trousers. The three of us couldn't help but laugh our b*****ks off. I remember commenting that the wet patch looked like a map of Italy. This would not look good on the wedding photographs 😖.

Mick decided to sit on a nearby low brick wall. He spread his legs apart facing the sun in an attempt to dry out. The taxi came almost immediately. We got in. Mick fully opened the window. Another idea of his to dry his damp patch. He even tried breathing on it for the duration of the five-minute journey!

Once we had arrived in the Village, I told Mick there was a strong powerful hand dryer in the Gents toilets. This would certainly dry him off. Mick went to the gents. Lee, David and myself headed for the bar. There was no way I was getting caught in the gents with Mick legs apart looking like he was trying to s**g the hand dryer 😲.

We got our beer and sat down. Five minutes later, Mick enters the bar. Not a bad job of drying his pants really, but you could still see the yellow stained perimeter of Italy 😃. We all had a right good chuckle over it. As usual Mick laughed it off.

Lee was being sensible, sipping at a couple of single whiskeys. Mick was Mick! Me and our David got in a round with him. All three of us got a round in. This was in less than an hour. Lee left our company to stand outside. His bride to be was due shortly.

I told Mick to get to the toilet to empty his bladder again. The ceremony would take a while. He would be stood up for a while. It would not look good if he was p*****g himself during the ceremony right in front of the vicar 😆. Mick went to the toilet. Me and our David went outside to wait for the bride turning up. There were plenty of people waiting outside having a fag, basking in the beautiful sunshine. A few minutes later, out walks Mick 🙁.

His photo sensitive glasses immediately turned dark in the strong sunshine. He was holding a lit cigarette. His smart dickie bow was now distorted to one side. His top three shirt buttons were undone plus another couple of buttons near his belly were open. His trouser zip was half way down, but worse of all, he had a massive damp patch on the left-hand-side of his groin area this time! He'd done it again 😲. This time it looked like a map of Africa! I wasn't bad at geography in school! I told Mick to sit on the small wall facing the sun to dry out. We got Mick relatively smartened up again. Well, the best we could anyway.

It wasn't a pretty sight, but me and our David were dabbing him down, pulling up his zip, fastening a few buttons here and there, straightening his dickie bow, carnation etc.

He had a good ten minutes drying out before the bride turned up in the wedding car. Me and our David returned to the bar. I couldn't bear looking at my mate Mick, the best man to his brother Lee, walking into the ceremony with p**s stains on both legs. One shaped like Italy, one shaped like Africa 😄.

I met up with Mick the following day. As usual we had a right laugh! Honestly, nothing phases Mick. Apparently, all the wedding photos that included Mick were shot from his waist upwards 😄.

YOU COULDN'T WRITE IT 😄.   R.I.P. LEE ☐.

Damp Mad Mick does best man!

GRUMPY GRANDAD GED

My Mam has always, and still does, keep an assortment of toys at her house for when visiting family and friend's kiddies pop in. She likes to keep them entertained (another word for quiet 😊). One story in particular she told me, made me giggle.

When he was three or four, my nephew, Warren junior (My brother Warren's son), loved to pretend he was a shop owner whenever he visited or stayed over at Mams. He would set up his corner shop in the kitchen, very much like Arkwright's corner shop in Open All Hours 😊. He would have a small table as his counter. A little jewellery box for his cash till, containing Monopoly paper money and plastic coins. He made his own signs from old Christmas cards. He made two larger ones. Using a thick magic marker, the signs read OPEN and CLOSED. Using some plasticine, he would stick whichever sign was applicable onto the front of his counter. He had a small plastic chair behind the counter where he would sit waiting for customers. His shop sold pretend absolutely everything! Warren loved it. It kept him occupied for hours on end.

The problem was, the shop needed plenty of customers to keep Warren amused. Everyone that entered the house (I mean corner shop), had to buy some things. Doesn't matter what you needed. Warren sold it! You could buy spuds, carrots, newspapers, sweets, tea, coffee, a rocking horse, three-piece suite, a yacht! You name it, young Warren sold it 😀.

After you had bought goods, you would pay in Monopoly notes. Warren would serve you and give back your change. Everybody bought goods from Warren's corner shop 😀.

One day my Mam had to nip out for an hour. My brother Warren Senior drove her. This left my stepdad Ged (God rest his soul ☐), in charge. He was left alone with Warren Junior for an hour. That particular day, Ged was in a bit of a grumpy mood. He was not the best shopper in the world, plus it was Saturday. He studied and picked his horses out on Saturday mornings!

As usual the shop was opened all hours. Everything was neatly laid out. The OPEN sign was put up. All set up for the day's business 😀.

"Grandad!.....Grandad!......Grandad! What do you want to buy from the shop Grandad?" Came shouts from the kitchen (I mean corner shop). Ged got up a few times and bought some goodies in between trying to pick his horses out for the afternoon's racing. Ged loved to concentrate on selecting his losers 😊. The shop orders were relentless! Ged was getting grumpier by the minute!

An hour later, Mam and Warren arrived back home, each carrying full shopping bags.

Mam entered the living room. "Everything alright?" She asked.

"Yeh, no problem," answered Ged. He instantly made his way upstairs to get ready for his visit to the bookies and Saturday afternoon booze with his mates in the pubs of Manchester City centre 😊.

Warren was sat quiet on the couch looking glumly down with his arms folded. His eyebrows were crushed together, his bottom lip was out. He was clearly not a happy chappie 😠.

"What's the matter?" Asked his Nanna.

"I had to close the shop." He sulked.

"Why?"

"Grandad bought everything in the shop. He gave me a hundred pounds and bought everything I had!" 😕.

Mam and Warren couldn't help but laugh. Ged had deviously thought of a way out of getting mithered whilst he was trying to pick his horses. He had bought all of the contents of the pretend shop with pretend money.......Genius! 👍

YOU COULDN'T WRITE IT 😄.

Grumpy   Grandad   Ged ! 😦

Seeing as it's the last story, I'll throw another quick one in for free. 😃. Another one with Ged.

HANDS ON GED

My Mam and her beloved husband Ged went on many holidays together, both in Britain and abroad. This story Mam told me was during a trip to the Rock of Gibraltar. As a lot of people know, the Rock of Gibraltar is famous for the permanent occupation of the mischievous Barbary tail-less monkeys. These monkeys are little mischievous b*****s all the time 😖. They get up to all sorts of antics. They run around free. They jump on people. They nick food, bags, hats phones etc. Anything loose, they have it away. They are forever flying all over the place causing chaos 😫. Rumour has it, if the monkeys leave, it will bring the downfall of Gibraltar. So they are left free.

On the day Mam and Ged visited the top of the Rock of Gibraltar, workmen were carrying out maintenance and repairs. They were replacing signs, painting barriers and whitewashing walls. There were warning signs all over the place. 'Beware of your belongings'. 'Beware of the monkeys. 'Beware Wet Paint' and 'Beware Whitewashing in progress'.

There were the usual kids running around shouting and screaming at the monkeys with disgruntled parents trying to keep them in check 😖. Mam reckons there were well over fifty monkeys flying all over the place, causing alarm and panic to the tourists who were all nervously trying to safeguard their belongings 😖.

Mam noticed something strange. Although there was wet paint and whitewash everywhere, not one of the monkeys had a speck of paint on them 😕. It was if they could read the signs? She looked around. Not one of the kids had a drop of paint on them either?

Mam was really intrigued at the fact that not one monkey or kid had a single blemish on them 😕. Was it the colour or smell of the paint? She remarked on these facts to Ged. She commented on how small their brains (monkeys and kids) must be. She joked the apes must be able to read in English and Spanish! She was fascinated. All this time, mam presumed Ged was behind, listening.

"Brenda!....Brenda!"

Mam was all too used to this loud voice shouting over. She turned around. Yes, you've guessed it! Ged was stood with both arms stretched. Both palms and arms were covered in white paint 😖. There was whitewash all down the right-hand side of his shirt and smart trousers. Mam didn't know whether to laugh or cringe in embarrassment. She ended up laughing her head off 😅. Ged was the only living thing on the rock of Gibraltar with paint on him! Not only that, he was covered in it, head to foot 😄.

YOU COULDN'T WRITE IT ! 😅 .   R.I.P. GED. GOD BLESS !

I hope you have enjoyed these short, absolutely true stories. I know there are many more stories out there. If you would like me to write on any of your personal funny experiences, please do not hesitate to let me know. Write your story to me via email or WhatsApp.

If you enjoyed this short book, please give it a good review on Amazon. Please send me a photo of you holding the book or better still, have a photo taken with me and yourself holding the book.

One last favour. If you don't mind. Please can you tell me your personal favourite three stories in order, first second and third. I have different people telling me their different favourites. It's very interesting knowing different opinions😃.

Thank you so much for following and reading my work. You are genuinely appreciated.

Keith.

keithhealiconbooks@gmail.com

Printed in Great Britain
by Amazon

39063392R00066